This Is a Let's-Read-and-Find-Out Science Book®

Revised Edition

A Drop of Blood

by Paul Showers • illustrated by Don Madden

THOMAS Y. CROWELL NEW YORK

LET'S READ-AND-FIND-OUT BOOK CLUB EDITION

The *Let's-Read-and-Find-Out Science Book* series was originated by Dr. Franklyn M. Branley, Astronomer Emeritus and former Chairman of the American Museum–Hayden Planetarium, and was formerly co-edited by him and Dr. Roma Gans, Professor Emeritus of Childhood Education, Teachers College, Columbia University.

Printed in the United States of America. For information address Thomas Y. Crowell Junior Books, 10 East 53rd Street, New York, N.Y. 10022. Published simultaneously in Canada by Fitzhenry & Whiteside Limited, Toronto.
1 2 3 4 5 6 7 8 9 10
Revised Edition

Library of Congress Cataloging-in-Publication Data

Showers, Paul.
A drop of blood / by Paul Showers ; illustrated by Don Madden. — Rev. ed.
p. cm. — (Let's-read-and-find-out science book)
Summary: A simple introduction to the composition and functions of blood.
ISBN 0-690-04715-0 : $.
ISBN 0-690-04717-7 (lib. bdg.) : $
1. Blood—Juvenile literature. [1. Blood] I. Madden, Don, 1927- ill.
II. Title. III. Series. 88-3623
QP91.S525 1989 CIP
612'.11—dc19 AC

A Drop of Blood

There is blood everywhere inside your body. When you cut yourself, you make a hole in your skin. Blood leaks out through the hole. If the cut is small, it soon stops bleeding.

Oh, there's blood in your arms and your legs,
There's blood in your fingers and toes,
And once in a while
When a game gets too rough,
You'll find that there's blood in your nose.

You don't have to cut yourself—or bump yourself—to find out where blood is. You can *see* where it is.

You can look at your blood with a flashlight.

Go into the bathroom tonight and shut the door. Turn on the flashlight in the dark. Hold your fingers over the light. What color are they?

Look in the mirror in the dark. Hold the flashlight behind your ear. What color is your ear? Shine the flashlight in your mouth. What color are your cheeks? The blood in your fingers and your ear and your cheeks makes them look red.

Blood is red because it is full of tiny red cells. They float in a watery fluid called plasma. The red cells are very tiny. There are hundreds—and thousands—and millions—of them in a single drop of blood.

Red cells are too small to see with your eye. You have to look at them under a microscope. Then the red cells look like this—round and flat, thin in the middle, thick around the edge—something like tiny doughnuts without any holes.

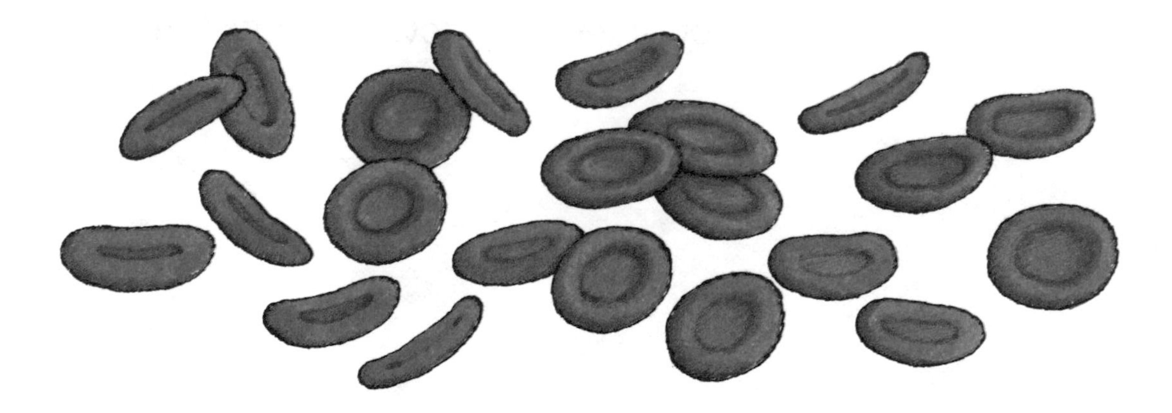

The blood is always moving inside your body. Your heart pumps it and keeps it moving. It moves through little tubes—your blood vessels. It moves out to the tips of your fingers. It moves up to your head and down to your toes.

The red cells carry oxygen. Oxygen is part of the air you breathe. You cannot see oxygen, but you cannot live without it. Your body has to have oxygen every minute. You breathe oxygen into your lungs. The red cells in your blood take the oxygen from your lungs. Red cells carry the oxygen to every part of your body.

They carry oxygen to your muscles—to your bones—your brain—your stomach and intestines—your heart.

muscle
bone
brain
heart
lungs
stomach
intestines

Your body needs food as well as oxygen.

When you eat, the food goes down to your stomach and your intestines. There food is changed into a fluid. The fluid moves from your intestines into your blood. You cannot see the food anymore, even under a microscope. But it is in your blood.

Your blood takes the food and oxygen to every part of your body. It takes food to your bones to make them grow, to your muscles to make them strong, to your fingers and your toes—even to your brain.

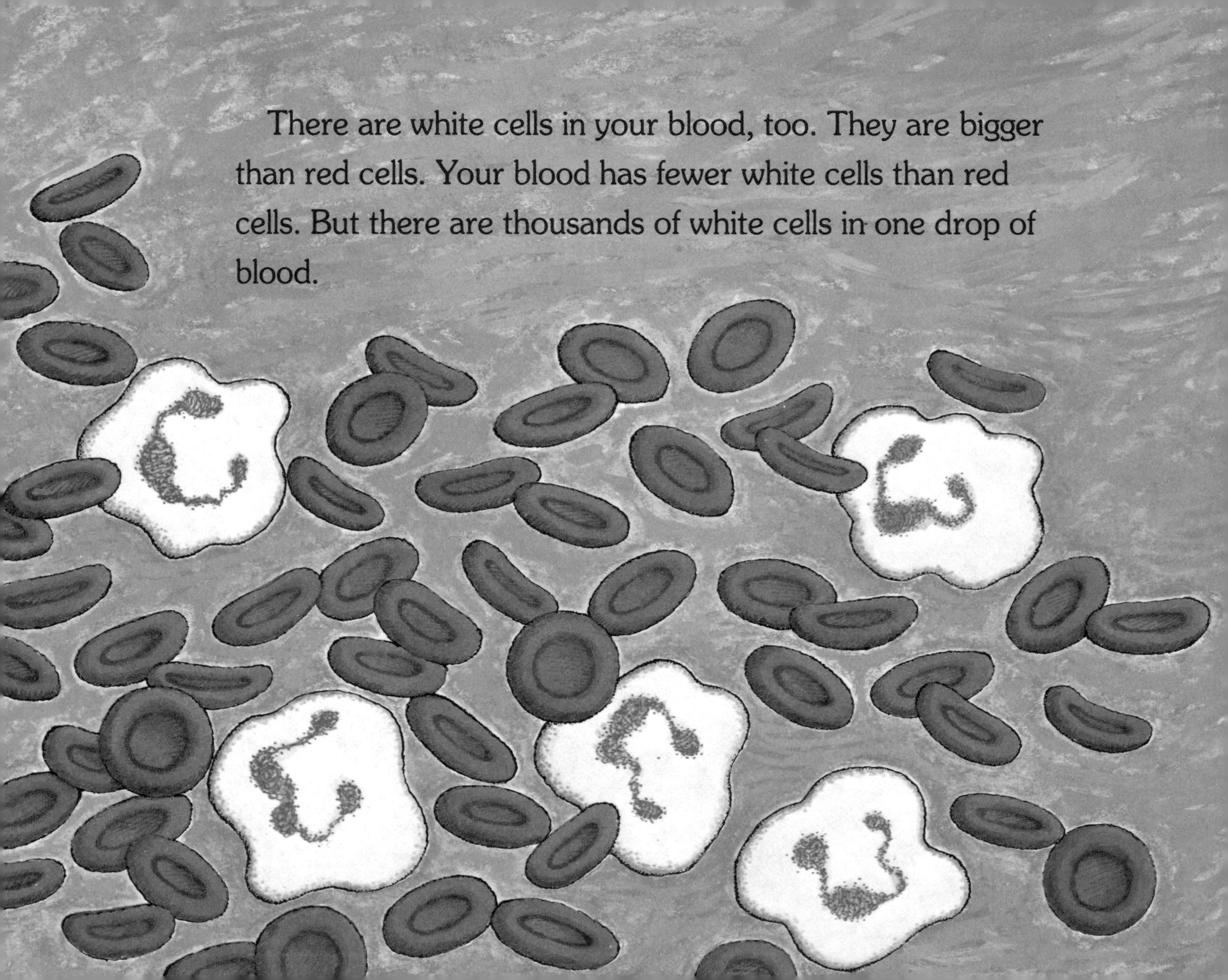

There are white cells in your blood, too. They are bigger than red cells. Your blood has fewer white cells than red cells. But there are thousands of white cells in one drop of blood.

White cells protect you against disease germs. A white cell wraps itself around a germ and eats it up. Then the germ cannot harm you.

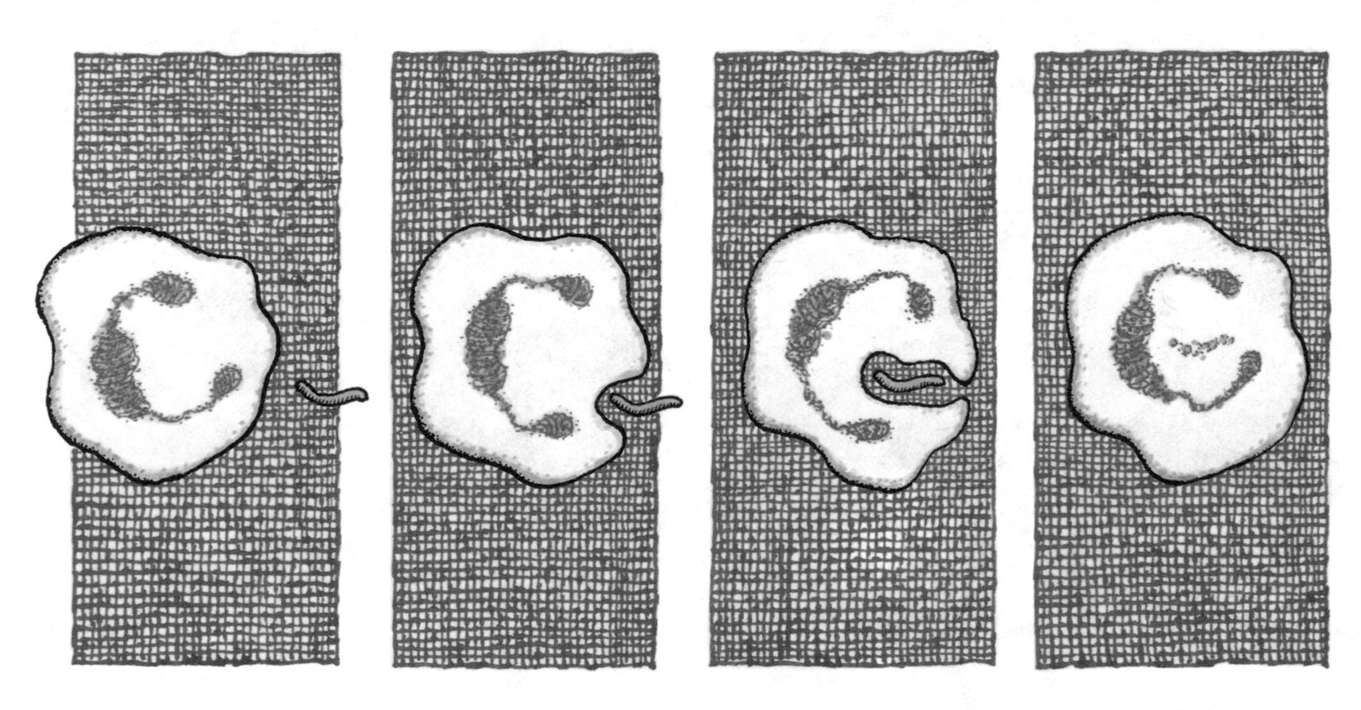

A white cell eating a germ.

Some things in your blood are smaller than the white cells—even smaller than the red cells. They have no color. They are flat and round, like little plates. They are called platelets.

When you cut your skin, blood runs out. Platelets gather around the cut. They form a plug that helps stop the bleeding.

Platelets pour in through the blood vessels to plug up the cut.

Next, the blood begins to clot. Tiny threads called fibrin form in the plasma. The fibrin threads make a net across the cut. Red cells and white cells are caught in the net. Soon the net becomes thick with red and white cells. A clot has formed. The blood cannot flow through the clot. The bleeding stops.

The clot hardens and becomes a scab. Later, new skin will grow under the scab and close the cut.

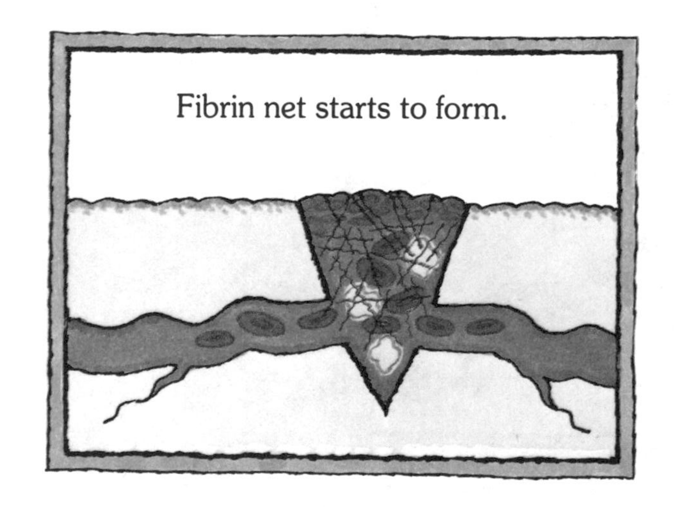

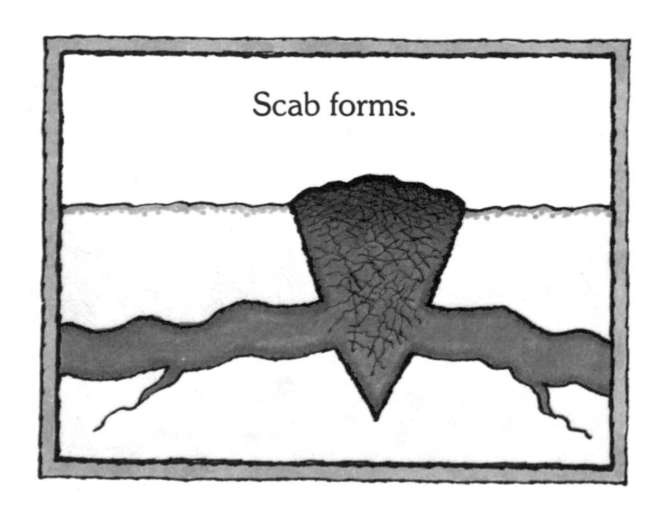

Little people do not need much blood. Cathy is one year old. She weighs twenty-four pounds.

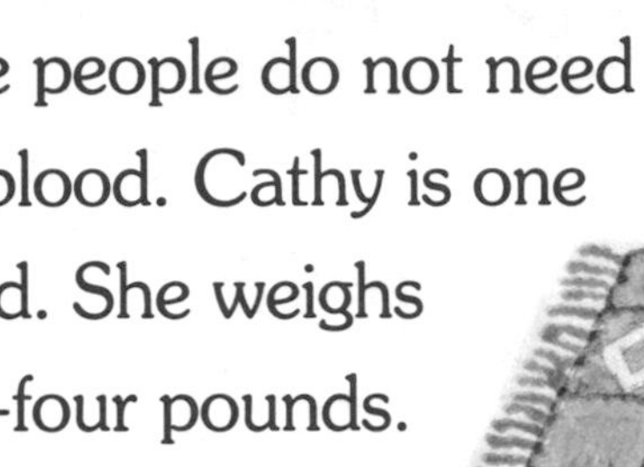

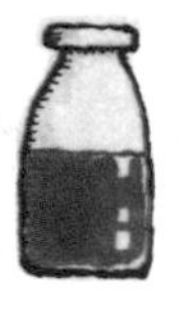

She has about one and a half pints of blood in her body.

That is less than one quart.

Big people need more blood. Russell is eleven years old. He weighs eighty-eight pounds. He has about five and a half pints of blood in his body.
That is a little less than three quarts.

=
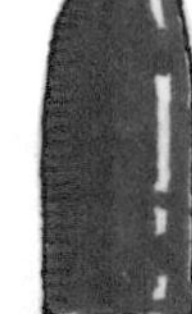

An adult who is six feet tall and weighs 180 pounds has about eleven pints of blood.

Eleven pints are the same as five and a half quarts.

Red cells do not last forever. They wear out. White cells and platelets wear out, too. But your body makes new red and white cells and new platelets every day.

When you cut yourself, you lose some blood. You lose red cells and white cells. You lose platelets. But that doesn't matter. Your body has plenty of new ones to take their place. It keeps making new ones all the time.

Relax, Rover—
It's no big deal!

Sometimes I cut my finger,
Sometimes I scrape my knee.
Sometimes a drop or two of blood
Comes dripping out of me.

That means I lose some platelets,
Some white cells and some red;
I lose them by the millions
In every drop I shed.

But I don't get excited
About my bleeding skin—
For all the blood that oozes **OUT**
There's plenty more that's **IN**.